facebook and
Instagram
Advertising:
for Businesses

written by
Joel Erlichson

Copyright

Table of Contents

Chapter 4: Navigating Facebook Advertising for Beginners

4.1: Setting Up Your Facebook Business Page

4.2: Facebook Ads Manager: A Comprehensive Guide

4.3: Creating Your First Facebook Ad Campaign

4.4: Analyzing Your Facebook Ad Performance

Chapter 5: Instagram Advertising: A Step-by-step Guide

5.1: Getting Started with Instagram Business Profile

5.2: Instagram Advertising Basics

5.3: Creating Your First Instagram Ad Campaign

5.4: Interpreting Your Instagram Ad Results

Chapter 6: The Art of Targeting: Creating High-Quality Leads

6.1: Understanding Audience Segmentation

6.2: Effective Targeting Strategies

6.3: The Role of Lookalike Audiences

6.4: Leveraging Customer Data for Advanced Targeting

Chapter 7: Converting Leads into Customers

7.1: Understanding the Conversion Funnel

7.2: Strategies for Increasing Conversion Rates

7.3: Lead Nurturing and Follow-Up Techniques

Chapter 1: Introduction to Social Media Advertising

1.1: Why Social Media Advertising?

In today's interconnected digital world, the key to reaching new clients and expanding your business's horizon often lies in leveraging the power of social media advertising. With over 3.5 billion active social media users worldwide, platforms like Facebook and Instagram offer businesses a vast ocean of potential clients waiting to be tapped into.

Unlike traditional advertising mediums, social media platforms offer a unique mix of extensive reach, precise targeting, interactive engagement, and comprehensive insights.

These platforms not only help you connect with a broad audience but also allow you to engage with them on a personal level.

Social media advertising can help you to:

- Increase brand awareness: By leveraging the vast user base of social media, you can introduce your business to a wider audience.
- Reach your target audience: With advanced targeting options, you can ensure your advertisements are seen by people who are most likely to be interested in your products or services.
- Drive customer engagement: Through likes, comments, shares, and direct messages, you can build relationships with your clients and foster loyalty.

- Measure and optimize: Social media platforms provide detailed analytics that allows you to measure the effectiveness of your campaigns and make necessary adjustments to optimize results.

1.2: Understanding Facebook & Instagram

Facebook and Instagram, two of the most popular social media platforms, offer businesses unique opportunities for client acquisition. Each platform has its unique features and caters to a slightly different audience demographic.

Facebook, with its diverse user base of over 2.8 billion monthly active users, is a versatile platform ideal for businesses of all sizes and types.

Its sophisticated advertising platform allows you to target users based on their location, age, gender, interests, and behavior. Facebook also offers different ad formats and placement options to suit your advertising goals, whether it's brand awareness, lead generation, or sales.

Instagram, on the other hand, is known for its visual appeal and is extremely popular among younger audiences. As of 2021, it had over 1 billion monthly active users. Instagram's advertising platform is integrated with Facebook, allowing you to enjoy the same targeting features. However, Instagram's emphasis on visual content makes it ideal for businesses with visually appealing products or services.

- Measure and optimize: Social media platforms provide detailed analytics that allows you to measure the effectiveness of your campaigns and make necessary adjustments to optimize results.

1.2: Understanding Facebook & Instagram

Facebook and Instagram, two of the most popular social media platforms, offer businesses unique opportunities for client acquisition. Each platform has its unique features and caters to a slightly different audience demographic.

Facebook, with its diverse user base of over 2.8 billion monthly active users, is a versatile platform ideal for businesses of all sizes and types.

Its sophisticated advertising platform allows you to target users based on their location, age, gender, interests, and behavior. Facebook also offers different ad formats and placement options to suit your advertising goals, whether it's brand awareness, lead generation, or sales.

Instagram, on the other hand, is known for its visual appeal and is extremely popular among younger audiences. As of 2021, it had over 1 billion monthly active users. Instagram's advertising platform is integrated with Facebook, allowing you to enjoy the same targeting features. However, Instagram's emphasis on visual content makes it ideal for businesses with visually appealing products or services.

As a business owner, harnessing the power of Facebook and Instagram advertising can open the door to a world of new clients. In the next chapters, we will delve deeper into how you can effectively utilize these platforms to grow your business.

Chapter 2: Basics of Advertising

2.1: What is Advertising?

In the context of Facebook and Instagram, advertising is the process of creating and publishing promotional content with the aim of reaching a targeted audience on these platforms. It involves the strategic use of visuals, text, hashtags, and user data to encourage desired actions, such as website visits, product purchases, or even simply building awareness about your brand.

2.2: Importance of Advertising for Your Business

Advertising on Facebook and Instagram holds significant potential for businesses of all sizes. Here are a few reasons why it's crucial:

Reach: These platforms house billions of active users, providing an extensive audience base.

Targeting: Their advertising systems allow for detailed targeting based on user demographics, interests, behaviors, and more.

Engagement: The interactive nature of these platforms allows businesses to engage with potential clients in a more personalized way.

Analytics: Detailed performance insights enable businesses to adjust and optimize their strategies based on real data.

2.3: Different Types of Advertising on Facebook and Instagram

Facebook and Instagram offer a range of ad types to cater to different business needs:

Image ads: These are simple yet effective ways to showcase your products or services.

Video ads: Video content can grab attention and are useful for demonstrating how a product works or telling a story about your brand.

Carousel ads: These allow you to showcase up to 10 images or videos in a single ad, each with its own link.

Slideshow ads: These are video-like ads made up of a series of static photos or videos.

Collection ads: These provide a visual and immersive way for businesses to showcase their products or tell their brand stories.

Story ads: These are immersive, full-screen ads that appear between users' Stories on Instagram.

Messenger ads: On Facebook, these allow you to engage directly with users through Messenger.

Each ad type serves different purposes, from building brand awareness to driving conversions, and can be leveraged according to your specific business goals.

Chapter 3: Exploring the Power of Targeted Lead Generation

3.1: Understanding Lead Generation on Facebook and Instagram

In the realm of Facebook and Instagram advertising, lead generation is a strategy used to attract and convert users into prospects or 'leads'. A lead is a potential customer who has expressed interest in your product or service by taking an action, such as filling out a form on your website, signing up for a newsletter, or engaging with your ad. The goal is to guide these leads through the marketing funnel to eventually become paying customers.

3.2: The Importance of Targeted Lead Generation

Targeted lead generation takes this concept a step further. Instead of casting a wide net with your advertising efforts, the focus is on attracting leads who are genuinely interested in and likely to engage with your business.

There are several reasons why targeted lead generation is vital on Facebook and Instagram:

- Efficiency: By focusing your resources on users who are most likely to convert, you can get a higher return on your ad spend.
- Relevance: Targeted ads are more relevant to users, providing a better user experience and increasing the likelihood of engagement.
- Better Conversions: High-quality, targeted leads are more likely to become paying customers.

- Improved Customer Relationships: Targeted leads often result in customers who are more satisfied with your product or service, leading to longer-term relationships.

3.3: How Targeted Lead Generation Works

Facebook and Instagram provide a wealth of user data that can be used for targeted lead generation. These platforms allow advertisers to create custom audiences based on a range of criteria, including demographics, interests, and behaviors. This level of segmentation ensures your ads reach users who are most likely to be interested in your product or service.

In addition to targeting ads, Facebook and Instagram offer lead generation ad formats designed to collect information from interested users directly within the platform. For example, Facebook's Lead Ads allow users to fill out a form with their details without leaving the app, reducing friction in the lead generation process and increasing the chances of conversion.

The power of targeted lead generation lies in its ability to use data and analytics to optimize advertising efforts, attract high-quality leads, and ultimately, drive business growth. In the following chapters, we'll delve deeper into how you can leverage this strategy in your own Facebook and Instagram advertising campaigns.

Chapter 4: Navigating Facebook Advertising for Beginners

4.1: Setting Up Your Facebook Business Page

Your journey to Facebook advertising begins with setting up a Facebook Business Page. This serves as your business's home base on the platform, where you can share updates, post content, and interact with your followers.

- Choose the right page type: For businesses, select 'Business or Brand'.
- Provide accurate information: Fill in your business name, address, and category.

- Customize your page: Add a profile picture (typically your logo) and cover photo that represent your business. Fill out the 'About' section with detailed information about your business.
- Invite followers: Start inviting existing customers, friends, and colleagues to like your page.

4.2: Facebook Ads Manager: A Comprehensive Guide

The Facebook Ads Manager is your command center for advertising on Facebook. It's where you'll create your ad campaigns, set your budget, define your target audience, choose your ad placements, and analyze your results.

- Navigate the Ads Manager: Learn the layout and functionality of this tool.
- Understand the campaign structure: Facebook ads are organized into three tiers – campaigns, ad sets, and ads.
- Explore the targeting options: Ads Manager offers a wide range of targeting options based on demographics, interests, behaviors, and more.

4.3: Creating Your First Facebook Ad Campaign

Creating your first ad campaign can feel like a big step, but Facebook's Ads Manager guides you through the process.

- Customize your page: Add a profile picture (typically your logo) and cover photo that represent your business. Fill out the 'About' section with detailed information about your business.
- Invite followers: Start inviting existing customers, friends, and colleagues to like your page.

4.2: Facebook Ads Manager: A Comprehensive Guide

The Facebook Ads Manager is your command center for advertising on Facebook. It's where you'll create your ad campaigns, set your budget, define your target audience, choose your ad placements, and analyze your results.

- Navigate the Ads Manager: Learn the layout and functionality of this tool.
- Understand the campaign structure: Facebook ads are organized into three tiers – campaigns, ad sets, and ads.
- Explore the targeting options: Ads Manager offers a wide range of targeting options based on demographics, interests, behaviors, and more.

4.3: Creating Your First Facebook Ad Campaign

Creating your first ad campaign can feel like a big step, but Facebook's Ads Manager guides you through the process.

- Choose your objective: Facebook offers several objectives such as brand awareness, traffic, engagement, app installs, video views, lead generation, and conversions.
- Define your target audience: Use the targeting options to define who you want to reach.
- Set your budget and schedule: Determine how much you want to spend and when you want your ads to run.
- Create your ad: Choose your ad format, and then add your images, videos, headline, description, and call-to-action.

4.4: Analyzing Your Facebook Ad Performance

Once your ad is live, it's crucial to monitor and analyze its performance. This allows you to see what's working and make data-driven decisions.

- Understand the metrics: Facebook offers a range of metrics like reach, impressions, click-through rate, conversion rate, and return on ad spend.
- Evaluate your performance: Regularly check your ad performance against your set objectives and adjust as necessary.
- Optimize for better results: Use your performance data to refine your ad campaigns, whether that means adjusting your audience, changing your ad creative, or modifying your budget.

This chapter is your roadmap to kickstarting your journey on Facebook advertising. In the upcoming chapters, we'll explore the dynamics of Instagram advertising and how you can harness its potential to boost your business growth.

Chapter 5: Instagram Advertising: A Step-by-step Guide

5.1: Getting Started with Instagram Business Profile

Before you can start advertising on Instagram, you'll need to set up an Instagram Business Profile. This is your professional account on Instagram where you can share posts, stories, reels, and IGTV videos, and where you can engage with your followers.

- Setting up your profile: You can either convert an existing Instagram account into a business profile or start from scratch. Provide all relevant business information.

- Customize your profile: Select an appropriate profile picture (usually your logo), write a catchy bio, and add a link to your website.
- Connect to Facebook: For advertising purposes, it's crucial to connect your Instagram Business Profile with your Facebook Business Page.

5.2: Instagram Advertising Basics

Instagram, now owned by Facebook, operates its advertising within the same ecosystem. This means that you'll use Facebook's Ads Manager to create and manage your Instagram ads.

- Understanding Instagram ad placements: Your ads can appear in the main feed, the Explore page, or within Stories.

- Exploring ad formats: Instagram supports several ad formats like photos, videos, carousel ads, and stories ads.

5.3: Creating Your First Instagram Ad Campaign

Creating your first Instagram ad campaign involves a similar process to Facebook, with a few additional steps:
- Choosing your objective: As with Facebook, the first step is to choose your objective in Ads Manager.
- Defining your audience: Tailor your audience for the Instagram platform.
- Placements: Make sure to select Instagram placements.

- Customize your profile: Select an appropriate profile picture (usually your logo), write a catchy bio, and add a link to your website.
- Connect to Facebook: For advertising purposes, it's crucial to connect your Instagram Business Profile with your Facebook Business Page.

5.2: Instagram Advertising Basics

Instagram, now owned by Facebook, operates its advertising within the same ecosystem. This means that you'll use Facebook's Ads Manager to create and manage your Instagram ads.

- Understanding Instagram ad placements: Your ads can appear in the main feed, the Explore page, or within Stories.

- Exploring ad formats: Instagram supports several ad formats like photos, videos, carousel ads, and stories ads.

5.3: Creating Your First Instagram Ad Campaign

Creating your first Instagram ad campaign involves a similar process to Facebook, with a few additional steps:

- Choosing your objective: As with Facebook, the first step is to choose your objective in Ads Manager.
- Defining your audience: Tailor your audience for the Instagram platform.
- Placements: Make sure to select Instagram placements.

- Creating your ad: Choose your format and add your creative content. Remember, Instagram is a visually-oriented platform, so make sure your ads are aesthetically pleasing and engaging.

5.4: Interpreting Your Instagram Ad Results

- After your ad has run for a while, you'll need to evaluate its performance:
- Understanding the metrics: Instagram offers metrics such as reach, impressions, engagement, clicks, and conversions.
- Analyzing your performance: Check your ad performance in Ads Manager and compare it to your initial objectives.

- Optimizing your ads: Use your performance data to improve your ads, whether that means adjusting your audience, testing new creative, or increasing your budget.

By mastering Instagram advertising, you'll have another powerful tool at your disposal for reaching new clients. In the next chapters, we will delve deeper into advanced strategies and tactics for Facebook and Instagram advertising.

Chapter 6: The Art of Targeting: Creating High-Quality Leads

6.1: Understanding Audience Segmentation

Audience segmentation is the process of dividing your target market into distinct groups based on various criteria like demographics, interests, behaviors, and more. By segmenting your audience, you can create more tailored and effective ad campaigns on Facebook and Instagram.

The value of segmentation: ability to enable marketers to tailor their strategies and messages to meet the specific needs and preferences of different customer groups increasing overall business profitability.

6.2: Effective Targeting Strategies

For those who are new to advertising, targeting might seem daunting, but it's essential to ensure that your ads reach the most relevant audience. Here are some simple strategies that you can use:

Demographic and Interest Targeting: This is about showing your ads to people who fit specific criteria related to their personal characteristics, such as their age, gender, where they live, how much money they earn, or even what their hobbies are. For instance, if you're selling young adult novels, you might want to target teens and young adults who show an interest in reading.

Behavioral Targeting: This strategy involves targeting people based on what they've done in the past. For example, if someone visited your website but didn't make a purchase, you can show them an ad as a reminder or offer a special deal to encourage them to come back and buy something.

Geographic Targeting: This involves showing your ads to people in specific locations. For instance, if you have a local bakery, you'd want to show your ads to people who live near your store, not someone who lives thousands of miles away.

Time-based Targeting: This is about adjusting when your ads show up based on when your audience is most likely to be online.

If your target audience is working adults, for example, you might schedule your ads to run during lunch hours or in the evening when they're likely to be browsing online.

Understanding these strategies can help you reach the right people with your ads, and improve the success of your campaigns.

6.3: The Role of Lookalike Audiences

Lookalike Audiences are a powerful marketing tool provided by platforms such as Facebook and Instagram. They allow businesses to target users who are similar to their existing customers or high-value prospects. This feature works by leveraging the data you have on your current audience to find new prospects with similar characteristics, behaviors, and preferences.

What are Lookalike Audiences:
Lookalike Audiences are essentially a group of social media users that mirror the qualities of another group (your source audience).

This source audience could be based on your existing customers, website visitors, or even individuals who have interacted with your content or ads on Facebook or Instagram. The Lookalike Audience feature uses machine learning algorithms to identify commonalities among the source audience and then finds users with similar profiles.

How to create Lookalike Audiences: To create a Lookalike Audience, you'll first need to define your source audience. This could be a custom audience created from your website visitors, a list of customer email addresses, or users who've interacted with your Facebook or Instagram page.

Once you've defined your source audience, you can then select the option to create a Lookalike Audience in the audiences' section of Facebook or Instagram ad manager. You'll then be asked to choose the size of your Lookalike Audience (1-10%, with 1% being the most similar to your source audience) and the geographic area you want to target.

Best practices for using Lookalike Audiences: For the best results with Lookalike Audiences, it's advised to continuously update and refine your source audience to ensure it represents your ideal customer.

Additionally, since Lookalike Audiences are based on the data from your source audience, the larger and more defined your source audience is, the better your Lookalike Audience will be. Finally, regularly testing and optimizing your ads will help you maximize the success of your campaigns using Lookalike Audiences.

6.4: Leveraging Customer Data for Advanced Targeting

Both Facebook and Instagram offer capabilities to harness your existing customer data to fine-tune your ad targeting:

Custom Audiences: This involves the creation of a unique audience segment based on your current customer data. It's a way of directly targeting users who have a pre-existing relationship with your business.

Retargeting: This strategy involves using your Custom Audiences to display ads to individuals who have already interacted with your business in some way. It can be an effective way of re-engaging users who've shown interest in your products or services.

Integration of Custom and Lookalike Audiences: By strategically deploying both of these tools, you can extend your reach while maintaining a highly relevant target audience. This involves targeting not only your existing customers (Custom Audiences) but also individuals who share similar traits and behaviors (Lookalike Audiences).

Armed with knowledge and understanding of these targeting strategies, you'll be better prepared to generate high-quality leads through your Facebook and Instagram advertising campaigns.

Chapter 7: Converting Leads into Customers

7.1: Understanding the Conversion Funnel

A conversion funnel is a marketing model that illustrates the theoretical customer journey from the first interaction with your brand to the final purchase - converting a lead into a customer. It's particularly useful in digital marketing strategies, including Facebook and Instagram ads, as it allows marketers to tailor their efforts according to each stage of the customer's journey.

The conversion funnel is typically divided into three main stages - awareness, consideration, and conversion.

- The Awareness stage is when potential customers first learn about your business. This could be through seeing a social media post, ad, word-of-mouth, or any type of marketing effort.
- The Consideration stage is when these potential customers start thinking about whether your product or service can meet their needs. They might visit your website, read reviews, or compare your offerings with those of competitors.
- The Conversion stage is when these prospects decide to make a purchase and become customers.

Using the funnel: Understanding each stage of the conversion funnel can help you tailor your marketing efforts. In the awareness stage, your goal might be to increase your brand visibility. Thus, you could use broad-targeted ads or engaging social media content. In the consideration stage, you might focus on showcasing the unique benefits of your product or service, perhaps through testimonials or detailed product descriptions. Lastly, in the conversion stage, your strategy could involve incentives like discounts or limited-time offers to encourage the final purchase decision.

7.2: Strategies for Increasing Conversion Rates

Your conversion rate is the percentage of leads that become customers. Improving this rate is key for maximizing your return on ad spend. This section will cover various strategies for boosting your conversion rate:

- Optimizing your landing pages: Making sure the page where users land after clicking your ad is effective at converting them.
- Testing your ads: Using A/B testing to find the most effective ad elements.
- Retargeting: Using ads to re-engage users who have interacted with your business but haven't converted.

7.3: Nurturing Leads and Implementing Follow-Up Strategies

Transforming a lead into a customer involves not just capturing their interest, but also maintaining it and steering it towards a purchase. This process, known as lead nurturing, can be broken down as follows:

Understanding Lead Nurturing: Lead nurturing is the targeted engagement of a potential customer with the goal of fostering their interest and trust in your brand, eventually leading to a purchase. It plays a crucial role in maintaining connections with potential customers, keeping your brand top-of-mind, and steering leads towards a purchase decision.

Automated Follow-ups: Automating follow-up communications is an efficient way to ensure consistent engagement with your leads. This could include personalized emails, reminders about abandoned shopping carts, or notifications about new product updates or sales.

Content Marketing: This involves delivering relevant and valuable content to your leads. The objective is to build a relationship with your audience, establish your brand as an expert in your field, and keep leads engaged with your brand. This can include blogs, videos, infographics, and more.

Mastering these components will empower you to successfully convert high-quality leads into customers, thereby maximizing the effectiveness of your Facebook and Instagram advertising campaigns.

Chapter 8: Advanced Techniques for Facebook and Instagram Advertising

8.1: Exploring Dynamic Ads

Dynamic Ads are a sophisticated advertising strategy that automatically showcase your products to individuals who have previously shown interest, whether on your website, app, or elsewhere online.

Understanding Dynamic Ads: Dynamic Ads are a key feature of Facebook and Instagram that create personalized and timely ad experiences. These adaptable ads automatically use content relevant to a potential customer's expressed interests, leading to potentially increased engagement and higher conversion rates.

Creating Dynamic Ads: This section walks you through setting up your first Dynamic Ad campaign, which involves connecting your product catalog, defining the audience, and designing the dynamic template that will be filled with relevant product information.

Optimizing Dynamic Ads: Here you'll learn how to make the most of your Dynamic Ad campaigns. This might involve segmenting your retargeting audience, ensuring your product catalog is of high quality, and conducting tests to identify which ad elements are most impactful with your audience.

By gaining a deep understanding of these advanced advertising techniques, you'll be equipped to enhance the effectiveness of your ad campaigns on Facebook and Instagram.

8.2: Utilizing Facebook Pixel and Instagram Shopping Features

8.2: Harnessing the Power of Facebook Pixel and Instagram Shopping Features The Facebook Pixel and Instagram Shopping are potent tools that can elevate your digital marketing game. They allow you to monitor user behavior on your website and directly present your products on Instagram.

1. **Mastering Facebook Pixel:** Facebook Pixel is a piece of code that you install on your website. It collects data that helps you track conversions from Facebook ads, optimize ads, build targeted audiences for future ads, and remarket to people who have already taken some kind of action on your website.

We'll guide you through how it works, and how to set it up on your website.

Optimizing Instagram Shopping:
Instagram Shopping is a feature that allows businesses to showcase their products directly from their Instagram profile, posts, Stories, or even from Instagram's Explore section. We'll provide guidance on how to set it up and how to use it to engage effectively with your customers.

Enhanced Targeting with Pixel Data:
The data that the Facebook Pixel collects can be invaluable for refining your ad targeting strategy. This section will discuss how you can use this data to optimize your ad targeting, ensuring your ads reach individuals most likely to be interested in your products or services.

8.3: Retargeting: Reaching Out to Previous Site Visitors

Retargeting is a sophisticated strategy designed to recapture the attention of individuals who've interacted with your business online without converting into customers.

Understanding Retargeting:
Retargeting aims to reconnect with potential customers who've shown interest in your products or services by visiting your website, browsing certain pages, or adding items to a shopping cart, but left without completing a purchase. These users are already familiar with your brand, making them more likely to engage with your ads and eventually convert into customers.

Launching a Retargeting Campaign:
Initiating a retargeting campaign involves several steps. First, you'll need to set up a tracking tool, like Facebook Pixel, on your website to collect data on visitor behavior. Next, you'll use this data to create Custom Audiences of users who have interacted with your site. Finally, you'll create targeted ads tailored to this audience's previous interactions with your site, reminding them of the products or services they've shown interest in.

Perfecting Your Retargeting Efforts:
There are numerous ways to optimize your retargeting campaigns.

This could include segmenting your audience based on their behaviors (like users who viewed a particular product versus those who abandoned their shopping carts), personalizing your ad content to reflect the products or pages they interacted with, and testing different creative elements to see which perform best.

Equipped with a deep understanding of these retargeting techniques, you'll be prepared to reengage past visitors and improve the chances of converting them into customers.

Chapter 9: Maximizing Results with A/B Testing

9.1: Understanding A/B Testing

A/B testing, also known as split testing, is a way to compare two versions of an ad to find out which performs better. It's a valuable technique that can help fine-tune your ad campaigns on Facebook and Instagram.

Grasping the Essentials of A/B Testing: A/B testing is a controlled experiment where you change one variable in your ad (version A) to create a second version (version B), then measure which version achieves better results.

This could mean higher click-through rates, more conversions, or any other metric that's important for your campaign. It's a crucial part of campaign optimization as it enables you to make data-driven decisions, minimizing guesswork and assumptions.

Identifying Variables for A/B Testing: When A/B testing, you can change various elements of your ad to see how it impacts performance. This could include the headline, ad copy, images or videos used, call to action, targeting parameters, or even the time of day the ad is shown. It's crucial to only change one variable at a time, ensuring that any difference in performance can be attributed to that specific change.

By understanding and utilizing A/B testing, you'll be better equipped to maximize the efficiency and effectiveness of your Facebook and Instagram ad campaigns.

9.2: Implementing A/B Testing in Your Campaigns

The integration of A/B testing into your ad campaigns isn't just advantageous—it's crucial for enhancing and fine-tuning your advertisements.

Initiating A/B Tests: Starting A/B tests on Facebook and Instagram involves a few key steps. You'll need to select the campaign you want to test, create two versions of the ad set with one key variable changed, and decide the amount of your budget to allocate to each version. After running the ads for a certain period, you'll review the results to see which version performed better.

Determining Variables for Testing: Choosing which aspect of your ad to test depends on your marketing objectives. If you're looking to boost engagement, you might test different images or headlines. If you want to increase click-through rates, testing different call-to-actions could be beneficial. Remember, the goal is to isolate one variable at a time to accurately measure its impact.

As you become proficient in applying A/B testing to your campaigns, you'll be better prepared to optimize your ad performance based on concrete data, leading to more successful Facebook and Instagram campaigns.

9.3: Interpreting A/B Testing Results

After the A/B tests have run for a sufficient time, it's essential to study the data, draw meaningful insights, and apply those to enhance future campaigns.

Decoding Your Results: The outcomes of your A/B tests will yield a wealth of data, but it's crucial to know which metrics to focus on. Depending on your campaign goals, these could include click-through rates, conversion rates, cost per action, or engagement rates. The version of your ad that performs better in these key metrics is the one to move forward with.

Data-Driven Decision Making: Interpreting the data isn't just about identifying which ad version performed better.

It's about understanding why it performed better. Did a certain headline resonate more with your audience? Did a specific image or call to action drive more conversions? The insights gleaned from your A/B testing should guide your future ad design and targeting decisions.

By deeply comprehending A/B testing and its results, you can continually refine your Facebook and Instagram ad campaigns, assuring you extract the most value from your advertising budget.

Chapter 10: The Future of Social Media Advertising

10.1: Emerging Trends in Social Media Advertising

As social media platforms continue to advance, they bring new possibilities for advertising. Let's delve into some rising trends on Facebook and Instagram.

Augmented Reality (AR) and Virtual Reality (VR) Ads: AR and VR technologies are beginning to redefine social media advertising by providing immersive experiences. AR ads, for instance, might allow users to virtually "try on" products via their phone cameras.

Meanwhile, VR ads could immerse users in a 360-degree virtual environment, providing more engaging product experiences or brand narratives.

Video Content: The significance of video content in advertising continues to escalate. Short, engaging videos are increasingly prevalent on platforms like Instagram, and longer-form video content on Facebook Watch is on the rise. Given the high levels of user engagement with video content, advertisers are integrating it more frequently into their strategies.

Personalization and AI: With advancements in AI, ad personalization has become more refined and effective.

By analyzing user data, AI can help advertisers deliver more personalized and relevant ads, leading to improved engagement and conversion rates. Understanding these emerging trends will help you anticipate changes in the advertising landscape, equipping you to adapt your strategies accordingly and maintain a competitive edge.

10.2: Keeping Up with Changes in Social Media Platforms

Facebook and Instagram are perpetually evolving, regularly introducing new features and modifying their algorithms. Staying current with these changes is pivotal to harnessing their full potential.

Staying Informed about Updates: It's essential to keep track of the latest changes on Facebook and Instagram to stay ahead in the game. You can do this by following official blogs or news updates from Facebook and Instagram, subscribing to reputable digital marketing newsletters, or participating in online communities of social media marketers where such updates are often discussed.

Flexibly Adapting to Changes: Rapid adaptation to new features and algorithm changes is key to maintaining a robust advertising strategy. This could mean tweaking your ad content or design based on new ad features, or adjusting your targeting approach in response to changes in the platform's algorithms. Remember, the goal is to continually optimize your strategy to achieve the best possible results within the current platform environment.

Staying informed and adaptable will equip you to better leverage the ongoing changes in Facebook and Instagram, ensuring your advertising strategy remains effective and competitive.

10.3: Maintaining a Competitive Edge in Digital Advertising

The swift progression of digital technology necessitates foresight and adaptability in order to stay competitive in social media advertising.

The Pursuit of Constant Learning: In the dynamic digital landscape, it's crucial to commit to lifelong learning. This includes staying up-to-date with the latest social media trends, technological advancements, and changes in consumer behavior. Regularly attending webinars, reading industry publications, and participating in relevant forums can help maintain your knowledge.

The Importance of Experimentation: Implementing new strategies, tools, or ad formats and measuring their effectiveness is key to discovering what resonates most with your target audience. This could mean testing different types of content, experimenting with various ad placements, or trying out new targeting methods.

Anticipating and Adapting to Future Changes: Being able to anticipate trends and adjust your advertising strategy accordingly is crucial for longevity. This includes staying aware of technological advancements, predicting changes in consumer behavior, and preparing for shifts in the digital advertising landscape.

By staying informed, being willing to experiment, and preparing for the future, you can keep your business at the forefront of digital advertising, particularly on platforms like Facebook and Instagram.

Thank You

On behalf of the entire team at CalculatedLeads.com, I want to express our sincerest gratitude for your trust and engagement with our business. Your support means the world to us and it is you, our esteemed clientele, that drives our passion and commitment to delivering exceptional service.

We recognize the unique challenges and opportunities present in today's dynamic digital landscape. We also understand that, as a business owner, your time is precious and should be dedicated to what you do best - growing your business and creating value for your customers.

With this in mind, I'm thrilled to offer our PPC, SEO, and Automatic Appointment Setting services. Our advanced, targeted algorithms work tirelessly to locate high-quality leads that are actively looking for the unique solutions your business offers. Our service doesn't stop at lead generation - our automated system steps in to nurture these leads, scheduling appointments directly to your calendar, offering a streamlined, effective process that operates in real-time.

Each lead we deliver is exclusive and unshared, guaranteeing their potential is entirely yours to harness. We adhere to a strict policy of promoting only one business of a kind in a city, meaning you get unparalleled, localized attention.

We don't just offer leads; we're passionate about creating long-term, successful relationships that see your business thrive.

Should you wish to discuss this opportunity further, or if you have any questions or queries, our team is always available to assist. We're excited about the potential of partnering with you and aiding your business's growth through our refined lead generation and management services.

Thank you once again for your continued trust in CalculatedLeads.com.

Joel Erlichson